The feathers of
macaws
add colour to the forests

The deep blue colour of these two hyacinthine macaws (*Anodorhynchus hyacinthinus*) is not created by the presence of any particular pigment, such as carotene, but is simply the result of the way in which light is diffracted off the feathers.

THE LARGE PARROT FAMILY

A variety of different species are generally grouped together under the term parrot: macaws, Amazon parrots, budgerigars and cockatoos. These Psittaciformes (from the Latin *psittacus*, meaning parrot) have in common brightly-coloured feathers and a powerful beak. Macaws are among the largest members, growing up to one metre long, whilst budgerigars remain the smallest. Psittaciformes are native to every continent except Europe where they are now extinct, and are most common in the tropics.

Macaws (here *Ara macao* and *Ara ararauna*) are sociable and gregarious birds. They live in groups of around twenty, moving around in search of food.

Profile

The scarlet macaw
Ara macao
Family: Psittacines
Size: 80 cm
Weight: 850 g

Distribution: Central America and the northern half of South America
Habitat: dense forest
Diet: fruit, grain and nuts
Incubation period: 4 to 5 weeks
Number of young per brood: 2 or 3
Life expectancy: 80 years (more in captivity)
Distinguishing features: species threatened with extinction; trading is illegal

The parrot's beak is also used for moving around. When a macaw wants to move to a neighbouring branch, it grabs hold of it with its beak and one foot. This effectively gives it two footholds, enabling it to pull itself up with ease.

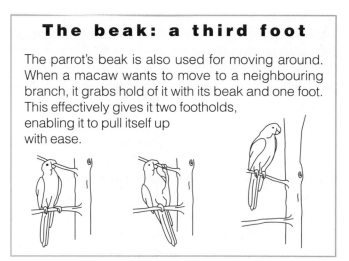

AMAZING POWERS OF IMITATION

Man has always been fascinated by the parrot's powers of imitation. The most gifted include the Amazon parrot, the macaws of South America, the grey parrot of Africa and the Australian cockatoos. In captivity, some are capable of reproducing words and sounds almost exactly. These skills are all the more surprising since there is no evidence to suggest that parrots reproduce the sounds of their natural environment in the wild. There they emit little more than raucous piercing cries. So why do they develop powers of imitation in captivity? Is 'speaking' a way for these otherwise gregarious and active birds to tackle the boredom and isolation of life in captivity? It is true that parrots kept as a pair learn to 'speak' less readily than those raised on their own, suggesting that this behaviour is indeed a way of establishing a closer link with humans in order to compensate for the lack of a partner.

Like all the macaws, this specimen of *Ara aracuna* has a very strong beak with razor-sharp edges, enabling it to chop up all sorts of fruit and seeds with astonishing ease. In the tropical forest, parrots are the only birds able to eat the tough plants.

As they worship the sun,
lizards
exhibit a wide range of colours

COLOURS TO SUIT ONE'S MOOD

Among the large family of colourful lizards, the prize of most colourful goes to the agamid. These large lizards, related to iguanas and chameleons, often exhibit wonderful colours, reflecting the mood of the moment (fear, aggression, sexual excitement…).

Almost all agamids live in very dry semi-desert regions of the world. Few live in humid conditions, unless it is also extremely hot. They are found in South East Asia, Australia, Africa, Asia and the Middle East. In Europe and America, however, they have been replaced by iguanas.

Other smaller lizards, such as emerald lizards and jewelled lizards, are equally brightly coloured but are incapable of changing colour. The male is usually a deep green, whilst the female is less vibrant and most often brown.

Profile

Lizards
Reptiles
Size: varies according to each species; from several mm to 50 cm

Distribution: all continents
Habitat: arid and semi-arid regions; occasionally humid regions
Diet: insects, eggs of other reptiles, other lizards
Predators: birds, small mammals

Most lizards need a great deal of heat which is why you often see them lying on stones and rocky surfaces, soaking up the sun. It is common for a group of them to sunbathe together.

The collared lizard, so called because of the black band around its neck, is a very strong agamid. When the rock on which it is lying becomes too hot, it raises its whole body so that none of it is touching the burning surface. This is essential when you consider that this lizard lives in the Australian desert where the temperature is always very high.

The colour of this agamid plays an important part in the regulation of its body temperature. Living in central Africa, its dark colours enable it to get rid of excess heat more quickly once it moves into the shade. Like its relative the chameleon, its colour also changes in order to frighten other animals, or when it is frightened itself or sexually excited. Here the agamid displays its mating colours.

The jewelled lizard is identified by blue eyespots on its flanks.

THE YOUNG ARE THE MOST COLOURFUL

'True' lizards (of the Lacertidae family) are found all over the world, from small Mediterranean islands to polar regions and the depths of Asia. All are oviparous: the female buries soft eggs underground. Once the young lizards have fully developed inside the egg, they break through the fine membrane and immediately start to fend for themselves. Initially their colours are much brighter than those of the adult, especially on the tail. These become less vibrant as the lizard gets older.

The emerald lizard (*Lacerta viridis*) has a wonderful bright green body and, in spring, a blue throat. It lives in southern Europe in a variety of areas, ranging from coastal regions to those at an altitude of 1600 metres. Only the male exhibits this green colour. The female is brown and much less vibrant.

With their long train,
peacocks
are the stars of the farmyard

ALL SET FOR A FASHION PARADE

Everyone knows of the spectacular feathers of the peacock: a metallic blue coat covers its neck and body, culminating in some 150 multicoloured longer feathers. This veritable palate of colour is spectacularly eye-catching. The blacks, browns and shades of red, orange and ochre are due to the presence, in various concentrations, of melanin, a dark pigment. The iridescence of metallic and golden reflections is, however, due to the diffraction of light, creating a seemingly infinite range of shades due to the shape of the feathers.

THE MOST MYTHICAL FEATHERS OF THE BIRD KINGDOM

In India, these rich colours have given the peacock the status of a mythical bird. Being a fearsome killer of cobras, the peacock is believed to obtain its colours from the poison of the snake. Due to this supposed immunity to the venom of the snake, the peacock has, in certain countries of the East, come to symbolize immortality.

Profile

Blue peacock
Pavo cristatus
Family: Phasianidae
Weight: 3.5 kgs–5 kgs

Distribution: India and Sri Lanka
Habitat: lightly wooded areas, close to water
Diet: buds, grain, shoots and small insects
Number of eggs per brood: 5 to 7
Life expectancy: 18 years (in captivity)
Incubation period: 28 days

The row of feathers on the blue head of the peacock look like knitting needles sticking in a ball of wool. The reason for these feathers, present in both the male and the female, remains a mystery, having no visible function in any of the peacock's courtship displays.

Contrasting with the blue of the neck, the strong green tail feathers help the male blue peacock to erect its famous fan of long feathers. The play of light on these feathers can change their colour, and the green and blue tones can momentarily appear black.

Very special feathers

The spreading of its tail is the most important part of the male peacock's courtship dance. The success of this display is made possible by the arrangement of the long feathers of the train. The longest, averaging 1.5 metres, are situated furthest down the back of the bird. At the end of each of these feathers is the famous eye-shaped design known as an ocellus because of its similarity with a small eye that has a dark pupil in the centre.

Turning back on itself, the male fans its pennae (long tail feathers) adorned with ocelli, which in turn reveal the green feathers at the back of its long neck, making it appear to swell out.

Noisy rustling

The visible attributes of the tail feathers depend on the direction in which they are facing. The male struts around for several minutes, helped in its endeavours to seduce by the noisy rustling that is produced as it shakes its feathers. And the female, feigning indifference, watches out of the corner of her eye, sizing up his abilities.

Extremely rare in the wild, albino peacocks are the result of genetic engineering. In certain animals, the white may sometimes be marked with black.

The peacock's train is not strictly speaking its tail: it is formed by feathers above the tail, known as upper tail coverts. Discrete but useful, the actual tail feathers act as a prop for the spread fan. The male has 20 fan feathers whilst the female, who does not use them in the same way, has only 18.

Fanned out, the train is like a shimmering tapestry, showing off the tail feathers to their best advantage. Given the lightness of these long feathers, the male is able to parade around for several minutes. If the female is seduced by the display, she squats down on the ground, inviting the male to mount her.

Light and graceful, fragile
butterflies
never cease to amaze

DELICATE COLOURS

Probably because of its wonderful colours, the butterfly is one of the most popular insects. Its scientific name Lepidotera (literally 'scaled wings') comes from the fact that their wings are precisely that, covered with thousands of small scales, overlapping like the tiles on a roof. Brightly coloured, they form wonderful vibrant patterns on the wings.

The colours themselves have different sources. Some come from various different pigments contained in the scales, others are the result of a simple physical phenomenon, the diffraction of light.

As all budding collectors will tell you, the colour of the scales is extremely fragile. If you handle a butterfly by its wings, the wonderful colours that create its beauty come off on your fingers, leaving little more than a trace of powder. So why not let these colours continue to flutter around in the wild instead of pinning them in some dusty old display cabinet?

A short life

As an adult, the butterfly has a very short life. The caterpillar can live for more than a year, but following metamorphosis, most types of butterfly only survive for a few days.
They pass this short life eating, feeding on nectar or other juices, and perpetuating the species.

In certain species, mating can last several hours. After a courtship display aimed at establishing that both partners belong to the same species, the actual mating can begin with the male sticking its abdomen against that of the female.

All butterflies, like this graceful *Graphium agamemnon*, often rest with their wings up, displaying their bright subtle colours.

The wonderful metallic reflections of this small pearly insect (*Issoria lathona*) are the result of light diffraction and not the presence of particular pigmentation. This small butterfly, common in southern Europe and north Africa, is a great migrator, travelling as far as Asia and eastern China.

Before flying off to discover the world from above, the swallowtail first makes sure that its wings are correctly unfurled. The rest of the chrysalis remains on the branch.

THE CATERPILLAR AND THE CHRYSALIS

The life cycle of the butterfly passes through four stages: the egg, the larva, known as the caterpillar, the chrysalis and the adult insect, or butterfly, usually with wings. The female lays groups of eggs on the plants that the caterpillar will feed on. When the eggs hatch, it is the caterpillar that comes out. Their three pairs of jointed legs, complete with claws, and the other pairs of false legs enable them to gain a secure grip on surfaces. Caterpillars spend their larval lives feeding on plants (some are even responsible for devastating entire crops). Their bright colours help to ward off predators.

After a certain amount of time, the caterpillar fixes itself to a stalk and spins a shell of silk around its body. Through the action of hormones, profound changes take place, giving birth to the chrysalis, which in turn produces the winged adult.

Close-up of a butterfly's wing. This shows clearly the thousands of small scales that give the wing its patterns and colours. Without these scales, the wing would be transparent.

Profile

Butterflies
Lepidoptera

Size: several cm

Diet: plants as a caterpillar, nectar and juice as an adult
Number of eggs per brood: from several dozen to several hundreds
Life expectancy: 1 to 2 years as a caterpillar, several days as an adult
Predators: birds, amphibians

In the limpid waters of the warm seas,
fish
perform their eternal multicoloured ballet

Clown fish (*Amphiprio bicinctus*) are famous for being able to live in harmony with sea anemone against whose poison they are immune.

COMMUNICATION BY COLOURS

According to many scientists, tropical fish are so brightly coloured because they live in a light environment. Tropical waters are often clear and light is able to penetrate far below the surface. In such transparent water, communication by colour (courtship, camouflage...) is of the utmost importance. This explains why in the less clear waters of somewhere like the North Atlantic, where sunlight can only penetrate the top few metres, the fish are much less colourful. The situation is even more extreme in caves and caverns where species are transparent or pale, given that colour brings no advantage in the battle for survival.

A shoal of 'masked' butterfly fish (*Chaetodon semilarvatus*). These small fish are among the most colourful that inhabit the coral reef. They spend the day exploring their domain in search of food.
At night, they sleep at the bottom and darken in colour slightly.

The colours of this angelfish (*Pomacanthus*) change according to its age. Angelfish, of the Chaetodontidae family, include a dozen or so different species, all of which are brightly coloured.

Tropical fish are colourful since they live in very clear waters. A second reason for this explosion of colour has, however, been put forward by some specialists. Given the profusion of species living in the tropics, colour is a way for them to tell each other apart.

With their black and yellow-striped jerseys,
wasps and hornets
are chic members of the insect world

On this thistle, a French paper wasp (*Polistes gallicus*) seems to be getting advice from some red bugs (*Pyrrhocoris apterus*). This type of wasp is very common in Europe where it is often mistaken for those wasps known as 'social' which are even more common.

NOT FIT TO EAT

Most of the species grouped together by the layman as wasps are in fact members of the same sub-family (Vespidae) of the Vespoidae family. They are classed as social species. In this group we find common wasps, whose bodies are never longer than 2 centimetres long, and hornets, certain female of which can be 3.5 centimetres long.

The bright yellow colour of wasps is a warning to predators, such as hedgehogs and birds, not to try and eat them. Wasps have a sting, a very poisonous 'needle'. Perhaps surprisingly, these weapons can bring benefits to humans — one thousand flies and caterpillars fall victim to each wasp!

This is what the head of the hornet, that large wasp with the much-dreaded sting, looks like from close up. The photo clearly shows its compound eyes and the famous segmented antennae which are used for touching and listening. Between its two eyes lies one of the three dorsal ocelli which serve as additional visual organs.

Hornets build their nests in hollow tree trunks or under the eaves of a house. The female breaks off tiny pieces of wood and uses them to build the nest. She mixes them together with saliva and uses the solution as a binder for attaching the first cells to the 'ceiling' of the hollow.

Dolichovespula saxonica lives under the eaves.

WINTER IN THE WARMTH

Social wasps are only seen when the weather gets warmer because they spend winter hibernating in a shelter, under the bark of a tree or in a crack in a wall. They wake during the first warm days of spring and begin to look for food, preferably the sweet nectar of flowers. Soon each female begins looking for a place to build a nest. This could mean an old tree stump, a bush, an attic or a hole in the ground, depending on the species.

Has one of these wasps found a fly in the ointment?
Is this a game or a fight?
Whatever the case, this battle between two wasps (*Dolichovespula media*) seems fierce.

The nest of *Polistes gallicus* is made from plant matter that has been chewed up and mixed with saliva. It consists of a single layer of cells attached by a strong stem to some support. The nest is abandoned once the larvae, which you can see here in some of the cells, have hatched out.

The wasp feeds using its mouth pieces. The two large yellow and black blades outside the jaw are used for chewing and tearing, whilst those on the inside (brown and hairy) are for licking and sucking up food. A word of warning: the insect is likely to take exception if you try to get as close as our photographer!

Despite having their beaks forever in the mud, the
flamingos
are nevertheless elegant waders

Throughout the world, different types of flamingo are not all the same colour. For example, this *phoenicopterus ruber ruber* – representative of a subspecies of flamingo from Central America – is slightly deeper in colour than its pink cousin and is known as the red flamingo along the northern coasts of South America as well as in Cuba, the Bahamas and the Galapagos Islands.

ENJOYING *LA VIE EN ROSE*

Few waders are as elegant as the flamingo thanks to its thin legs that seem to go on for ever, its long supple neck, the shape of its beak and its beautiful pink colour. This colour is all the more noticeable since flamingos live in large groups, numbering up to several thousand members. Everything it does is dominated by its membership to the group. The only time you are likely to see a flamingo on its own is if it is ill, weak or has escaped from captivity. Migration is also carried out en masse: twice a year, flamingos take off as a group, heading for a place to spend winter or build nests.

Being gregarious birds, flamingos remain as a group even when looking for food. In this way, each member can make the most of the mud being turned up by the whole of the group. As part of a group, they are also less at risk from predators: only a bird on its own, weakened by illness, tiredness or hunger runs the risk of being attacked, for example by a fox.

The black underside of the wings contrasts with the other feathers.

Profile

Flamingo
Phoenicopterus ruber
Wingspan: 1.6 m
Weight: male 3.5 kg,
female 2.5 kg

Distribution: southern Europe, central Asia, south-east Africa, the Caribbean and central America, the Galapagos Islands
Habitat: briny lagoons, salt-water lakes
Diet: small invertebrates, particularly *Artemia salina*, a small crustacean that gives it its colour
Mating season: spring (Europe)
Life expectancy: 35 years; 50 years in captivity

IT GETS ITS COLOUR FROM THE FOOD IT EATS

With the help of its long filtering beak, the flamingo continuously sifts the mud looking for small insects, worms, molluscs and crustaceans. It is, in fact, the latter that give the flamingo its pink colour. In the salt lakes favoured by the flamingo, a small crustacean, *Artemia salina*, lives in large numbers and it is this crustacean that contains a red pigment called carotene. This explains why only adult flamingos are pink – the young, fed on a liquid that is regurgitated by their parents and that does not contain much carotene, are a silvery-grey colour. It is only from the age of between six and nine months, when they have started feeding for themselves, that they begin to turn pink. In the past, flamingos kept in captivity used to lose their pink colour because of their diet. Nowadays, carotene-enriched food helps these beautiful birds to retain their colour, much to the pleasure of visitors to zoological gardens.

A beak used as a sieve

The flamingo's beak is used to sift mud. When the top moveable mandible, fitted with small horn-like growths, is brought down to meet the lower fixed mandible, edged with thin slats, they form a type of sieve that holds back all the small creatures in the mud that the bird moves around with the help of its thick tongue.

This coastal lake is an ideal habitat for the flamingo who will find the small crustaceans that make up its diet in the salt water.

Be they rigid or moving in the current,
coral, gorgonians and anemones
form a colourful underwater landscape

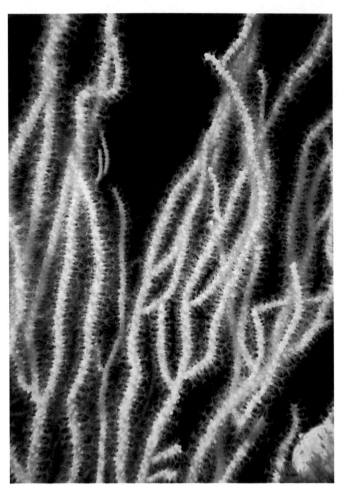

This yellow gorgonian is a fine example of the species *Eunicella cavolini*.

PLANT-ANIMALS

Coral, gorgonians and anemones, those veritable multi-coloured underwater bushes, are often thought of as plants. Even though they are fixed to the ocean floor, however, they are in actual fact animals, in much the same way as sponges.

Some (coral and gorgonians) are more or less rigid, consisting of a calcium skeleton on which the living parts, known as polyps, grow. Others, such as anemones, are completely flexible and consist of a mouth surrounded by many tentacles.

Red gold

The famous red coral (*Corallium rubrum*) has always fascinated humans who, seduced by its beautiful colour, took advantage of its exceptional hardness to us it in jewellery. As far back as Antiquity, coral was regarded as a precious stone and accorded special powers: the Romans carried it as an amulet or hung it round the neck of newborn babies to protect them from contagious diseases. The Gauls, on the other hand, crushed it and mixed it with wine to make a miracle cure.

Red coral (*Corallium rubrum*)consists of an external calcium skeleton (in red) full of small pores which enable the living part of the animal (in white) to open out in the current.

Some shrimps are immune to the poison of the anemone and live in perfect harmony with it, but this is not the case for *Leander serratus*: this shrimp is in the process of being digested.

This Dendronephtya is an alcyonarian coral, also known as soft coral, and is one of the most colourful types. The small rough growths that are clearly visible on its 'trunk' are small pieces of calcium known as spicules. These spicules serve as a skeleton and go some way to strengthening large soft coral which can grow to a length of one metre.

These small sea anemones certainly live up to their name of jewel anemones or pearl anemones. Large colonies cover huge rock surfaces, clothing them elegantly in colour. The colours vary wildly: green, blue, pink, yellow, purple, orange. Pearl anemones exist in all the colours of the rainbow.

Here, under the blue tentacles, you can make out the yellow 'foot' of this anemone.

POISON FOR KILLING THEIR VICTIMS

Related to the jellyfish, anemones, gorgonians and coral all kill their prey using urticating cells, known as cnidoblasts, situated on their tentacles. To catch their prey, they allow the current to spread out their tentacles in the water. As they come into contact with these long organs, unsuspecting small animals (crustacean larvae, small crustaceans, worms, fish eggs…) are immediately paralysed and carried towards the mouth by the folding action of the tentacles.

This fine example of *Balanophyllia regia*, a solitary coral some 2 centimetres high, is found in the Atlantic and the Mediterranean, anywhere between the surface and a depth of 50 metres. This species, which inhabits well-lit rock faces, spreads out its tentacles like the climax of a firework display.

A disguise helps
crab spiders
when they go hunting

One of the few spiders able to change colour at will.

COLOURS FOR CAMOUFLAGE

Camouflage is not only used in the animal kingdom by those wanting to hide from their predators. It is also used by the hunters themselves, such as many insect-eating spiders, especially members of the crab spider family, or Thomisidae. Their bright pink, green and yellow colours are a perfect match for the flowers on which they live, enabling them to lie in ambush. Some are even able to change colour to match a particular flower. This takes some time, but significantly increases the size of their hunting ground. Once camouflaged, the spider lies in wait for insects that come gathering pollen and nectar. As soon as the insect has its head turned, the spider leaps out at it and injects it with its poison.

The skull and crossbones on the back of *Synaema globosum* serve as a reminder of the strength of the poison of the European spider. It is a powerful neurotoxin which kills insects with lightning speed. Once the insect is dead, the spider makes a hole in its body and sucks out its innards.

This caterpillar is not having much luck and is going to end up as lunch for the crab spider.
A slow mover, the insect was taken by surprise whilst quietly feeding on a leaf.
Like many small spiders, this one is not afraid to take on prey that is much bigger than it.

It is not easy for an insect to tell the difference between the petals of this flower and the small spider that is lying in wait.
Most of the two thousand species of Thomisidae are found in the tropical forest, with only a hundred or so,
such as this *Thomisus onustus*, living in Europe.

This spider does not look to be very well camouflaged, but its green colour makes it almost invisible on the stalk of the flower. The camouflage is all the more effective given that the hairs on the body and legs of the spider are a perfect match for those on the plant.

Like multicoloured missiles, **kingfishers** animate rivers and lakes

An iridescent flash cuts through the air and nose-dives into the water: the spectacle of a kingfisher hunting. Its small body and short legs enable it to penetrate the surface of rivers and lakes, as do its thick orange and blue feathers which have the waterproof and thermal qualities necessary for a life spent in constant contact with water.

THE FEMALE AND THE MALE ARE EQUALLY BEAUTIFUL

The kingfisher lives on the quiet banks of rivers and lakes in Europe and Asia. The water itself must be clear to enable this bird, which lives solely on fish and aquatic insects, to see its prey. The kingfisher's appearance is unmistakable, with its small body, short neck, large head, long pointed beak, small tail and legs and, of course, the wonderful oranges and blues of its feathers. The beak, which is slightly redder in females, is the only way of telling the two sexes apart.

In spring, the kingfisher begins digging away at the bank with its long beak. The hole that it makes will serve as a nest for the female who lays six or seven eggs. Until the chicks leave the nest, after three or four weeks, they are completely dependent on their parents who fly back and forth several times a day to bring fish to their offspring.

Dropping from its perch, the kingfisher, with its beak slightly open, beats its wings to speed up its descent. Its piercing eyes have already spotted its prey and will remain locked onto it until it is caught. The kingfisher is equally impressive in water, thanks to its powerful muscles which enable it to adapt to the different elements.

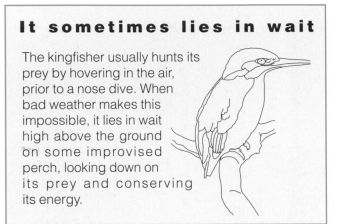

The kingfisher usually hunts its prey by hovering in the air, prior to a nose dive. When bad weather makes this impossible, it lies in wait high above the ground on some improvised perch, looking down on its prey and conserving its energy.

A SKILFUL PLAY OF LIGHT

The orange of the kingfisher's breast and the contrasting metallic blue of its back have different sources. The orange is due to the presence of organic pigments of the carotenoid family. The different shades of blue, on the other hand, are the result of the shape of the feathers themselves. Some of the small hairs that form the feathers, known as barbules, lie in such a way as to refract light so that only blue can be seen. This is why the bird's metallic colours vary according to the amount of light and the angle at which it is seen.

ENFORCED WINTER MIGRATION

In the northern and eastern part of Europe, as well as in central Asia, harsh winters and frozen water force the exodus of kingfishers towards coastal or southern regions. Some birds have been known to travel 800 kilometres from their native habitat

You win some, you lose some! This kingfisher has just missed its prey. In general, six out of ten attempts are successful following a 'hovering' attack. The bird is somewhat less skilful when it has been lying in wait, catching fish only four times out of ten.

Small fish form the main part of the kingfisher's diet. Occasionally, it will also eat insects such as dragonflies and coleopteran, batrachians, frogs and tadpoles. The kingfisher returns to its perch (a branch, post or reed) with the catch in its beak and beats it to death on a branch.

More emotional than calculating,
chameleons
are no master of disguise

Like all its cousins, the chameleon is a skilled climber. On the ground, it moves carefully and slowly but as soon as it is in a tree or bush it becomes agile and elegant. The incredible way in which it is able to contort its body with the aid of its tail is reminiscent of the lemurs of Africa and Madagascar and the sloths of South America.

ITS COLOUR CHANGES WITH ITS EMOTIONS

Contrary to popular belief, the chameleon does not always change colour purely as a way of camouflaging itself. These changes are in fact a reflection of its emotions. While resting, the animal – yellow or green – blends in perfectly with the foliage, but this is not the case as soon as it feels threatened: it becomes very pale when angry or red when it is anxious. Similarly, brown and yellow stripes appear when it is frightened. However, chameleons can imitate their surroundings, when they are immobile, and some even adorn themselves with spikes and horns: quite a range of defenses for a relatively small creature!

This chameleon, looking like something from prehistoric times, is surveying its territory. Its large eyes protrude and can move in all directions and independently. At the back of its head, the bony ridges from a sort of helmet.

As well as changing colour according to their moods, chameleons can also 'inflate' themselves. Here, this South African chameleon will not allow anyone on to its territory, not even our photographer who it is undoubtedly trying to frighten off.

The Parson's chameleon (*Chamaeleo parsonii*), native to the island of Madagascar, remains a little-known species which turns blue in certain situations. The animal can reach up to 60 centimetres in length and is identifiable by the two rostrums at the end of its nose.

In the guise of an owl or a tree trunk,
moths
know how to trick their enemies

INTIMIDATION AND CAMOUFLAGE: OPPOSITE SIDES OF THE SAME COIN

Next to butterflies, moths often seem rather insipid. Whilst it is true that their colours and patterns are slightly less vibrant, they are in themselves highly varied and are as equally interesting as those of the butterfly. Nothing, of course, happens by chance in nature and the variety of their colours and wing shapes is for several reasons: to ward off predators or be able to hide in foliage. On the inside of the wings, the ocelli (eye-shaped patterns) of certain moths are reminiscent of owls' eyes. Small birds, thinking that they are about to enjoy a peaceful bite to eat, are often forced to draw back at the last minute, seeing a large terrifying owl rise up from nowhere. It is usually on the outside of the wings that the pattern duplicates the bark of trees or the veins of leaves. All the moth has to do is spread its wings to go unnoticed.

Profile

Moths
Lepidoptera
Heterocera

Wingspan: 2 cm to 30 cm
Habitat: plains, agricultural areas, forests, mountains, swamps…
Diet: nectar from flowers
Life expectancy: several days as a moth
Predators: birds
Distinguishing features: longer wings than butterflies, highly developed antennae, sturdy body, often downy

Instantly identifiable by its long tail, the Indian luna moth (*Actias selene*) is a superb bluish green colour. The photograph shows the four ocelli characteristic of the luna moth.

This Atlas moth, the largest of the moth family, spreads its wings to display the elaborate pattern of reds and browns, undoubtedly aimed at frightening off the photographer who it sees as some type of predator. This large moth is found in southern Asia and the South Pacific.

The caterpillar of *Dasychira pudibunda*.

THE CATERPILLAR'S BRIGHT COLOURS

The caterpillars of moths are often brightly coloured. Once again, a number of reasons explain this: their colours are, of course, for camouflage but they also serve to intimidate and frighten off predators. The contrast of black with a bright colour (particularly orange or yellow) is often a warning to predators that an animal is poisonous. And in this case, they would do well to be cautious. Some caterpillars give off a corrosive liquid and others have urticating spines that will stick in an attacker.

Close-up of the head of an Indian luna moth. The antennae are a beautiful bluish-green, the same colour as the wings. Thanks to their highly sophisticated shape and the fact that they are covered with thousands of small olfactory sensors, the moth can detect the smell of a sexual partner from several kilometres.

Caterpillars are often more brightly coloured than the moths that they eventually change into.
This is the caterpillar of the Indian luna moth which lives on a large number of deciduous trees and shrubs.
It is found in countries from India, Sri Lanka and China to Malaysia and Indonesia.

A male pheasant at the beginning of the mating season

Sensitive harlequins,
pheasants
let love go to their heads

LOVE SWELLS ITS HEAD

The ring-necked pheasant might only be a distant cousin of the peacock, but its feathers, in the male at least, are equally as beautiful and have been worn in hats for many years. Like a carnival mask, red skin (or the caruncle) with almost no feathers surrounds the brilliant amber eyes of the male. As for the neck, it is an iridescent shimmer of colour ranging from blue to green. It is during the mating season, which begins in April, that male pheasants are at their most elegant: the caruncle becomes brighter and the two tufts of feathers at the back of the head, known as auricles, become erect. During the courtship display, the head swells out inordinately, making them look like overweight Casanovas.

Unlike male pheasants whose nuptial plumage has elegant metallic tints, female pheasants are a more modest brown colour. These discrete tones make it easier to go unnoticed while hatching the eggs.

This male pheasant, surveying his territory with an anxious eye, stands out wonderfully against the snow-covered field. Its anxiety is totally justified since, against the white background, the bird is an easy target for hunters.

During the courtship display, the male pheasant's head swells.

Profile

Ring-necked pheasant
Phasianus colchicus
Family: Phasianidae

Distribution: Asia, Europe, North America, New Zealand
Habitat: open woodland, fields with trees, thickets
Diet: plants, insects and small worms
Incubation period: 23 days
Number of eggs per brood: 8 to 14
Predators: humans and small mammals

FROM A PRINCELY DISH TO GAME

Native to Asia, the pheasant has always been considered a delicacy in the West. Introduced to Greece where it was reared for its meat, this succulent gallinacean was often on the menu at Roman banquets, and, slightly less flatteringly, was fed to circus lions. In the Middle Ages, monasteries and royal courts bred pheasants and the bird soon became princely game. The first pheasant hunts in the West began in the 12th century. By the 16th and 17th centuries, the sport had become so popular that certain German and English princes placed restrictions on the hunting of this wild bird. Today the pheasant is again one of the most hunted types of game, but thanks to intensive rearing programmes and the release of birds into the wild, the species is no longer threatened with extinction. Furthermore, they are now found in areas far from their native environment – they populate a large part of North America, as well as Hawaii and New Zealand.

An ancient history

The word 'pheasant' comes from the Latin phasianus, derived from the Greek word meaning 'inhabitant of the Phasis'. According to mythology, Jason and the Argonauts, in their quest to find the Golden Fleece, set sail for Colchis, a country situated on the east coast of the Black Sea (now called Georgia). There, on the banks of the river called the 'Phasis' (now called the Rioni), they are said to have seen the pheasant, for the first time. Tradition has it that they brought several specimens of this bird to their native Greece, and these became the first pheasants in Europe.

Each male ring-necked pheasant establishes a number of pathways across its territory and criss-crosses them frequently in search of food or possible intruders.

This dendrobate (*Dendrobates auratus*) has been photographed away from its favourite habitat: the trees of the equatorial forest. Like its other cousins, it lives off insects and earthworms, and is extremely poisonous.

The mating of two tree frogs. Some species never touch the ground, mating and laying their eggs in trees. They are often difficult to see among the vegetation due to their colour which can become deeper as night falls.

In the tropics, colourful
frogs
kill or hide

THE POISONERS OF THE FROG WORLD

Most tropical frogs are brilliantly coloured. Of these, the dendrobates of South America display the finest example of warning colours. And their predators would do well to take heed of this visual warning. These small frogs, which never grow more than 5 centimetres long, are capable of secreting a powerful poison through the glands in their skin.

In this family of poisoners, the prize for the most lethal goes to *Phyllobathes latinasus*, a small black frog with golden spots, which secretes the most deadly poison. Without any known antidote, this poison contains batrachotoxin, a powerful neurotoxin and a single gram of it is enough to kill 100,000 people!

The small speckled Hyperolius is found all over Africa, to the south of the Sahara and in Madagascar.
Well hidden on this big leaf, the little batrachian keeps its eyes open for a tasty insect to eat.
With a sudden flick of its sticky tongue, the frog will catch its prey in mid-flight.

The small strawberry frog (*Dendrobates pumilio*) does not live in fields of strawberries, but owes its name to the fact that it is the same colour and shape as the fruit. All the same, it is best not to confuse the two since this frog is a walking cyanide capsule.

The eggs of a tree frog, lying on a leaf. You can just see the tadpoles, protected from the air in their 'cocoon' of gelatine, waiting patiently to hatch.

Like many of its species, Hyperolius has a vocal sack that it inflates while croaking in order to attract females. Veritable recitals, given by many different species of frog take place at night. In the middle of this cacophony, each frog manages to pick out the distinctive croaking of a partner from the same species.

The highly poisonous *Dendrobates tinctorius*.

Men and frogs

For centuries, Amazonian Indians have extracted and used the poison of dendrobates. They roast them on a spit over a fire, collecting the poison that is released and ferment it. They then use it to cover the tips of their arrows which will paralyse and kill a bird or monkey as soon as it is hit.

A LICENCE TO KILL, BUT ALSO TO SEDUCE AND HIDE

The colours of certain frogs are not simply there to warn that they are poisonous. They also have other functions.

For tree frogs, their colours also serve as camouflage. The shades of green enable them to move around unnoticed among the foliage in which they live.

For others, bright colours help the male of the species to seduce the female.

Small adhesive pads lie at the ends of the fingers of *Hyperolius pleurotaenia*, a frog that passes most of its time in trees, preventing it from falling from leaves and branches.

The beauty of the male
birds
of paradise

An Emperor William's bird of paradise.

A male magnificent bird of paradise (*Diphyllodes magnificus*) cleans the area in which its courtship display will take place in the forests of New Guinea. Depending on the species, the display can take place on the ground or at different levels in the tree. The highest displays occur some 20 metres in the air.

GOOD LOOKS AND SEXUAL SUCCESS

Nowhere is sexual inequality so blatant as among birds of paradise. Whilst the males proudly display their magnificent colours, the females have to make do with drab brown feathers. Without exception, the males of 43 species of birds of paradise are all resplendent in their shimmering bright colours, from yellow and green to blue and red, not forgetting purple and violet. The fact that the males have long ornamental feathers, known as courtship feathers, whilst the female has none simply adds insult to injury. And to cap it all, even the eyes of males are brightly coloured: a golden yellow in Raggiana birds of paradise, a deep blue in the six-plumed bird of paradise. The females, however, do not hold any of this against the males. Quite the

With its wings spread and its chest puffed out, the Raggiana bird of paradise (*Paradisaea raggiana*)
struts about on a branch some 20 metres off the ground.
Begun with the first rays of daylight, this magnificent display is often repeated at nightfall.

The small king bird of paradise with its two courtship feathers.

Profile

**Raggiana bird
of paradise**
Paradisaea raggiana
Size: 15 cm, plus a
20-cm tail
Weight: 150 g to 200 g
Distribution: Papua New Guinea
Habitat: forests to an altitude of 1800 m
Diet: fruit-eaters, insect-eaters
Incubation period: from 13 to 15 days
Number of young per brood: 1 or 2, that
leave the nest after a month.
Life expectancy: between 10 and 15 years
Number: unknown, but falling

opposite. The more colourful the male, the more interested the female and it is with the most handsome that the females choose to mate.

BRIGHT COLOURS
MEAN A HEALTHY MATE

This preference for bright colours has nothing to do with aesthetics and birds of paradise are far from being the only creatures to favour this method of 'sexual selection': many female birds and fish choose their mates because of their bright colour. This is because the most brightly coloured are also the healthiest and the most resistant to disease. It is therefore natural that the female should choose them since they are being selected for breeding qualities and the female wants to ensure that she will have young that are equally strong and healthy. This is why when a group of males parade around a single female, as with the Raggiana bird of paradise, it is the female who chooses. And no prizes for guessing which will be the winner. The most colourful of course!

Fashion victims

The fashion for collecting birds of paradise reached its peak in the 19th century, when feathers were all the rage in Europe. The feathers of a Raggiana bird of paradise would fetch one pound sterling, whilst those of a blue bird of paradise could reach anything up to twenty pounds, a huge amount at that time. In 1913, the German part of Papua New Guinea alone exported 10,000 birds of paradise a year. In London, tens of thousands of birds a year were imported to decorate women's hats. World War II and changes in fashion put an end to the business, but trading still continues today, in spite of the fact that it is illegal.

Even the inside of the beak is colourful in some species of birds of paradise. Here the yellow is as important as the blue marking to the success of the courtship display.

The somewhat misleadingly named red bird of paradise (*P. rubra*).

THE EGGS ARE ALSO COLOURFUL

The eggs of the bird of paradise are among the most beautiful in the world. Laid one or two days after mating takes place, they too are colourful, ranging from orange and cream to shades of red and pink.

They always have lavender, grey, brown or reddish marks on them, perfectly spread out along the length of the egg, becoming darker at the widest part and completely disappearing at either end.

The male waigeu bird of paradise (*Cicinnurus respublica*) is one of the most colourful of all the species. Turquoise, electric blue, red and yellow: these colours could well be those of a country's national flag.

Courtship is a form of endurance test and the males use up an incredible amount of energy trying to show off their various colours. Some make a point of shaking their feathers, others become veritable acrobats. While all this is going on, the females, perched on neighbouring branches, make their choice. The males also accompany their movements vocally, letting out loud piercing cries.

The salamander has smooth shiny skin.

The larva of the salamander, identifiable by its large flat head with external gills. During the four months before metamorphosis, it is found frolicking around in pond water, artificial lakes, brooks or underground streams.

Two-tone
salamanders
have a bad reputation

HANDLE WITH CARE

The bright yellow markings on the black back of the salamander (*Salamandra salamandra*) are a warning to predators to keep their distance if they do not want to be incapacitated by the poison of this small amphibian. Some who are immune to the poison, however, choose to ignore this warning, viewing the salamander as something of a delicacy. This is the case of the hedgehog and the grass snake.

On the surface of its skin, the salamander has several different types of gland responsible for producing pigment, mucus to keep the skin moist, and poison. The poison is not harmful to humans, but it can irritate your eyes if you rub them after handling the animal.

Sometimes orange and black, the land salamander has fascinated humans throughout the ages. Because of its mysterious colours, its night-time activities and its sudden appearance after heavy rain, it was accused in the Middle Ages of being venomous and of poisoning the water in streams. An undisputed fiend.

Some 15 to 20 centimetres long, the salamander is often found in damp woods where the ground is covered with moss and where it can hide under stones and in old tree trunks. It is not unusual to find salamanders in caves, but you will never come across them in water. Even though it is born in water, the adult salamander is a weak swimmer and drowns easily.

It is odd to think that the most dangerous octopus of all is not some gigantic monster from the bowels of the earth but rather a minute and magnificent small colourful jewel. Colourful and very poisonous.

Beware of colourful
octopuses,
they may be poisonous

THE MASTER OF TRANSFORMATION

The octopus has a skill that is unique in the animal kingdom. It is able to change colour in a fraction of a second thanks to chromatophores (small cells containing pigment) in its skin. These highly specialised cells are able to contract and dilate, changing the concentration of pigment in them and thus altering the general colour of the whole animal. The result is an almost perfect form of camouflage against any colour of background. The octopus also uses this ability to change colour to frighten off potential predators, such as conger and moray eels.

Profile

Poisonous octopuses
Hapalochlaena maculosa
Hapalochlaena lunulata
Family: Octopoda
Size: 10 to 20 cm
Distribution: Australia and the Indonesian Archipelago
Habitat: shallow coastal waters
Life expectancy: 1 to 2 years
Distinguishing features: a bite from either of these octopuses is lethal

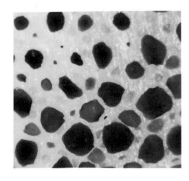

This close-up of the skin of an octopus shows the chromatophores, the cells responsible for its ability to colour. Whilst octopuses are only born with 65 of these cells, they will have between one and two million by the time they are a year old.

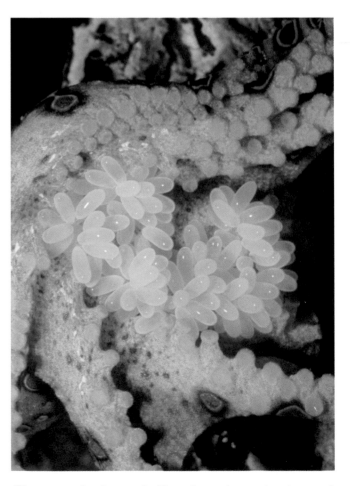

The octopus lays its eggs, in 10-centimetre long strings, in a crack in a rock, sheltered from predators. In all, the female lays between 100,000 and 500,000 eggs which she watches over carefully.

ONLY TWO SPECIES ARE DANGEROUS

The octopus has a bad reputation, fuelled by the many legends and stories told by sailors. Novelists have often portrayed it as a fearsome monster. In reality, the vast majority of octopuses are harmless and can even build up close relationships with divers.

Only two small octopuses are poisonous: *Hapalochlaena lunulata* and *Hapalochlaena maculosa*. Identifiable by the blue rings on their skin, these octopuses, which live in the tropics, are both able to blend into their environment, presenting an added danger for man. A child or a curious swimmer runs the risk of being lethally bitten since the poison in this bite is extremely powerful, causing sickness, a blurring of vision and breathing difficulties which can lead to a heart attack.

The blue rings of the Hapalochlaena warn predators of its extreme toxicity. When it feels threatened, the blue circles become iridescent whilst the colour of the rest of the animal becomes darker. Humans also need to beware of the bite of this small poisonous octopus.

The mating season lasts from April to August for the ibis. Both parents spend 21 days watching over two to five eggs in a nest built in a tree. When they are born, young ibis do not share their parents' scarlet colour

Crustaceans give
scarlet ibises
their striking colour

SOME ARE REDDER THAN OTHERS

Of all the different species of ibis, only *Eudocimus ruber* is bright red in colour. The other representatives are mostly white and black. Like its distant cousin the flamingo, the scarlet ibis is so coloured because of the food it eats, a similar diet of small red crustaceans. Naturally, the final colour of the animal depends on the concentration of these crustaceans in the mud that it filters. It is in fact quite common to find ibis that are pale pink. Similarly, young ibis are a brownish colour due to the fact that their diet is not the same as that of their parents.

Profile

Scarlet ibis
Eudocimus ruber
Family:
Threskiornithidae
Size: 50 to 90 cm

Distribution: the north-eastern coast of South America
Habitat: mangrove swamps, marshland, estuaries, lagoons
Diet: insects, molluscs, worms and crustaceans
Distinguishing features: a gregarious bird

The scarlet ibis lives in large colonies, often alongside other species of bird. Opposite, a group of scarlet ibis take flight with a flock of little egrets (*Egreta thula*) in a tangle of red and black.

The four fingers of the scarlet ibis (one at the front and three at the back) enable it to hold on to branches easily, as it does above, overlooking a mangrove swamp.

The scarlet ibis sifts through the mud of the mangrove swamp.

A THREATENED SPECIES

The scarlet ibis, with its tasty flesh, almost became extinct in the middle of the 20th century, the victim of too much hunting. In 1953 it became a protected species, enabling its numbers to 'move out of the red', no pun intended! The species is, however, still threatened with extinction in some parts of the world, such as in Guyana where only one breeding ground remains. Hunted without any restrictions, the number of nesting couples has fallen in ten years from a hundred thousand to just a hundred.

Like its cousins on other continents, the scarlet ibis has a long beak that curves downwards at the end. This is its best asset when it comes to feeding in any environment. It serves as an effective filter in the silty waters of the mangrove swamps and as a useful spade for digging up the ground in search of insects and small worms. It is also able to carry branches used to build the nest.

Tiny colourful jewels,
cuckoo wasps
live as parasites on other wasps and bees

It is on the back of its shell, and more precisely on the external side of the thorax, that the cuckoo wasp's most beautiful colours are found. The metallic tints are not the result of the presence of particular pigments, but rather are created by the diffraction of light.

TINY HARLEQUINS

Like tiny jewels among the Hymenoptera (wasps, bees, ants…), cuckoo wasps, also known as Chrysididae, have a wonderful metallic finish. Among the two thousand species of cuckoo wasps, the European varieties are by no means the least colourful: their blues, greens and ruby red hold their own against the deep purple of tropical species. Cuckoo wasps live as parasites on the eggs of other hymenopteran, in particular those of some bees and burrowing wasps. This is why they are often found in the nests of their host.

Cuckoo wasps are solitary wasps that live exclusively as parasites on other hymenopteran. While a wasp or bee is away, the cuckoo wasp enters its nest or hole and lays one or several eggs next to the larvae of its host. As soon of these have hatched, the parasitic larvae of the cuckoo wasp turn their attention to the host larvae which they eat before the latter have chance to metamorphose.

This pose is typical: in order to avoid being harmed by the host wasp, the cuckoo wasp rolls into a small ball and pretends to be dead, offering only its hard shell to the sting of its enemy. As it lies lifeless, it is just a matter of time before the host wasp throws it out of its nest.

This is the most common example of the European potter wasp. The female parasitic *Eumenes coarctata* is a solitary wasp and is often found on leaves and flowers since it loves the honeydew secreted by greenflies. But you need good eyesight. The insect is less than 5 millimetres in length!

With their multicoloured beaks,
puffins
live up to their nickname of 'sea parrots'

A beautiful beak is an essential part of the mating game. It is those with the most colourful beaks, both male and female, that will be the most successful during courtship. The beak also has another function: that of a tool for digging out a hole in the cliff face in which the couple will live and build a nest.

A COLOURFUL FALSE BEAK

From the same family as the penguin, the puffin differs from its cousin by the large multicoloured beak that it has in summer when it comes to mate on the rocky coasts of the North Atlantic.

During that period, a horny case grows over the beak in bright colours that send out important sexual signals. In autumn, the case falls off, leaving a beak that is smaller and with the same pattern in duller colours. In large numbers, the puffin then leaves the cliffs and heads out to the open seas for a period of several months.

During the mating season, gregarious puffins huddle together on the edge of cliffs. They rest, lying on the ground, for several hours a day, or wait standing up to follow one of the others as it takes flight.
In September, they fly off together to regain their fishing areas on the open sea.

Luckily, puffins do not suffer from vertigo…

Profile

Puffin

Fratercula arctica
part of Alcidae family
Size: 47 cm to 62 cm
Weight: 305 g to 675 g

Distribution: the North Atlantic
Habitat: rocky coastlines (from May to September) and the open sea (from September to May)
Diet: fish (sand-eels, herrings…), shrimps
Incubation period: 39 days
Number of young per brood: 1
Life expectancy: upto 21 years

AN EXCELLENT UNDERWATER SWIMMER

Not content with spending seven months of the year out at sea without touching dry land, the puffin spends most of its time in the ocean. There, it feeds itself and carries food to its offspring.

It catches its prey on or near the surface of the water: by beating its short wings vigorously, it can travel up to 50 metres under water, catching several fish during the same dive. On the menu: sand-eels, herring, sprats, capelins, mackerel, whiting, cod and haddock.

To complete its diet, it also manages to catch the odd shrimp. For that, it has to dive deeper to a depth of around 15 metres. The puffin is so dependent on the sea that it is extremely rare to find it inland. The exceptions tend to be birds that have been blown off course by a violent storm.

Like most sea birds, the dense feathers of the puffin are completely waterproof; essential for a bird that spends the entire winter at sea.

The puffin only carries food about to feed its young. To prevent the slippery catch from escaping, the tongue and palate are covered with small growths.

When not blending in with the scenery,
snakes
can be highly colourful

The golden snake, also known as the flying snake because its acrobatics performs, is a common sight in Australia.

COLOURS WHICH ALLOW THEM TO GO UNNOTICED

Like many other species of animal, snakes have developed colours to camouflage themselves, enabling them to hunt in secrecy and avoid undesirable meetings with predators and other snakes.

The colours of snakes vary according to the environment in which they are found. Thus, greens predominate in tropical forests whilst rock tones are more common in the desert. The colours tend to be brighter in younger members, as is the case with lizards.

Playing dead

Some snakes that are not lucky enough to be coloured in a way that enables them to camouflage themselves adopt a different solution when faced with an animal that is threatening them. They 'play dead' and at the same time give off a foul smell. The predator soon loses interest in this unappetizing find.

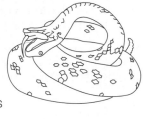

This king snake (Lampropeltis) is an almost harmless constrictor. It eats small rodents, lizards, birds, and even other snakes, be they poisonous or not, which it kills by wrapping itself around them and strangling them. It can grow to a length of 1 metre.

Spot the intruder! This small Philotamnus blends in with the green of the vegetation to avoid danger. A further attribute is that it resembles a very dangerous snake, the green mamba.

An emerald tree boa from South America.

Poison: a formidable weapon

Of over 3000 species of snake that have been listed, around 10 percent are of danger to humans. Their weapon: the formidable poison fangs, fixed to the upper jaw or folded back against the palate and thrown forward as the snake bites. Other species, such as the spitting cobra, can send their poison several metres. If this comes into contact with the eyes, it can blind.

ENEMIES ARE HANDSOMELY WARNED

It is clear that the colours of some snakes are not used as a way of camouflaging themselves in foliage or under rocks. They are also used to warn potential enemies that their owner is dangerous and best avoided. These warning colours enable the snake to reduce its chances of being attacked, at least during the day. They are of little help when faced with a nocturnal predator, such as an owl.

The arboreal snake (*Boiga dendrophila*) with its blue-black markings surrounded by yellow is found in Asia, Indonesia, and the Philippines. Whilst it lives mainly on birds, it is still dangerous to humans and several unfortunate encounters have been reported in Malaysia during recent years.

This snake of the genus *Lampropeltis* is a completely harmless but crafty little thing. Its skin is almost identical to that of the coral snake – an extremely venomous creature found in the deserts of South America. As *Lampropeltis* lives in the same countries as its dangerous model, it avoids its enemies, who thrown by its similarity, keep a respectful distance.

Elaphe obsoleta obsoleta is found in North America, Florida, Georgia and South Carolina.
It lives in copses, around swamps and in old buildings,
eating rodents and birds and attacking hen houses in built-up areas.

Like underwater flowers,
Sea slugs
decorate the ocean floor

A Hypselodoris with its branchial plume (at the back) open.

THE MAGIC OF COLOUR

Classed as gastropod molluscs, like the slug and the snail, nudibranches are found in almost all the oceans of the world. Their shape has earned them the name of 'sea slug', but unlike their less attractive land cousins, they come in all the colours of the rainbow, warning potential predators of their toxicity. These small animals, rarely more than a few millimetres in length, have gills and papillae (small spines) on their back covered with urticating cells. To some extent protected by their beauty, these sea slugs can cross coastal waters in complete safety.

A couple of Trapania maculata. No larger than 20 millimetres in length, these nudibranches were photographed in the Mediterranean, but are also found along the coasts of the English Channel and Brittany.

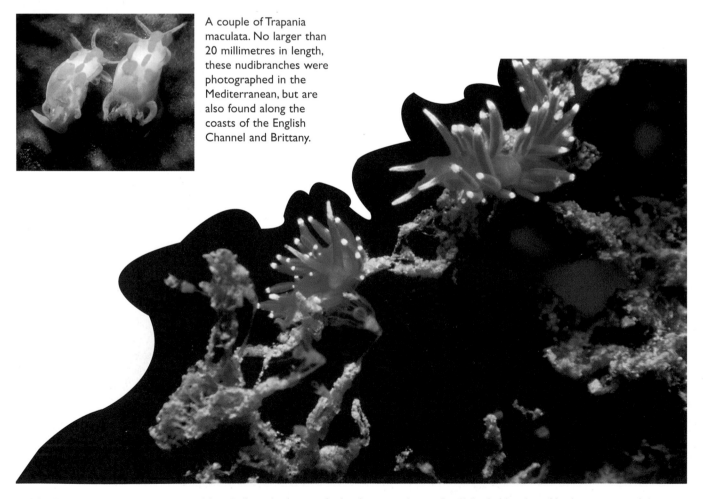

With all papillae flying, two sea slugs (*Coryphella pedata*) meet. Is this for courtship or food? Probably a bit of both.
Their search for the same things to eat has brought them together and it is not out of the question that they will take advantage of the chance meeting to further the species.

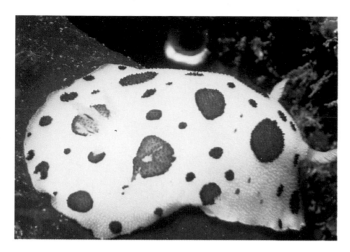

The exception: *Discodoris atromaculata* is not very colourful.

Profile

Nudibranches
Phylum: molluscs
Class: gastropods
Subclass: opisthobranches

Size: several mm
Distribution: coastal waters of all the oceans in the world
Habitat: rocky, sandy or muddy seabeds
Diet: jellyfish, sea anemones, sponges (among others)
Mating season: all year round
Distinguishing features: undeveloped eyes, urticating papillae, antennae or rhinophores, no shell

EXPOSED GILLS AND TENTACLES

Nudibranches breathe through their skin or gills, neither of which is covered by a shell. In some, a branchial crown completely surrounds the anus at the back of the body. In fact, its scientific name comes from this very feature: nudibranche means 'exposed gills'. During mating or feeding, when the animal needs a lot of oxygen, the gills are completely open. At the first sign of danger, it protects them by tucking them away in a fold on its back.

At the front of the body, one or two pairs of 'antennae' or tentacles are used for touching. Usefully replacing the undeveloped eyes of the sea slug, they enable them to carefully explore different obstacles on the seabed (stones, seaweed, sponges…). Behind the tentacles stand the thicker ringed rhinophores, the organs of smell in these small colourful animals which decorate coastal waters like flowers.

A sting in the tail

Sea slugs are able to protect themselves by reusing the urticating cells of the animals that they eat (sea anemone, coral and small jellyfish), a peculiarity that is unique in the animal kingdom. The slug, immune to the poison in these cells, stores them in its papillae. Pity the fish that is a little too voracious. It will remember its encounter with a sea slug for a long time and will think twice before attacking it again.

Flabellina ischitana attacks this sea anemone or hydroid to eat the polyps (small circles in the photo) that it loves so much.

ENCOUNTERS AMONG THE SEAWEED

Nudibranches are hermaphrodites, that is to say they have both male and female genital organs, but cannot reproduce on their own. Two individuals are essential. During mating, which often takes place following a chance encounter among the sponges, seaweed or hydroids, two sea slugs stick to each other head to tail. Fertilization, which can take many minutes, is mutual; the male genitals of one deposit their sperm in the female genitals of the other and vice versa. There is no notion of fidelity between sea slugs, and the two go their separate ways once the mating is complete, ready to have other encounters.

Coupling   Eggs

A RIBBON OF EGGS

Each animal lays its eggs on a piece of seaweed or around an 'underwater bush'. The eggs, which can total three thousand, are surrounded by a thin membrane, and look like a long ribbon that has been rolled up. Its shape is always the same. Depending on the species of nudibranche, this ribbon can look like a small rose or a ring. When the eggs hatch, the larvae move upwards to where there is plankton, spending the beginning of their lives a few centimetres from the surface of the water. Following metamorphosis, they fall back to the bottom of the sea where they take on their final shape and don their wonderful colours.

In an explosion of colour, *Dondice banyulensis* makes its way proudly along the seabed.
This species of nudibranche is slightly larger than the average sea slug, growing up to several centimetres long.

Here, *Flabellina affinis* performs a balancing act on a hydroid. This species of nudibranche is one of the most common found in the Mediterranean, familiar to most deep-sea divers. Like other species, it lives at the bottom of the sea at a depth of no more than 100 metres.

Frigate birds live in groups on their native island.

Frigate birds are capable of travelling great distances over water. These birds have such a finely-tuned sense of direction that on certain islands in the South Seas, they are used to deliver mail in the same way as carrier pigeons.

To find a mate, **frigate birds** inflate a red airbag

ALL PUFFED UP

Like many birds, the female frigate bird is not very colourful. The male, on the other hand, has beautiful black feathers with green tints and, under its throat, a bright red pocket which it puffs out during the mating season. The red, however, comes in a number of different shades since frigate birds only acquire their final colour at the age of four to six years.

Where can you find these elegant birds with the forked tail? In the West Atlantic, between the coasts of Florida and Brazil, and in the Pacific, off the coast of Ecuador and in the Galapagos Islands. Some couples also nest on the islands of Cape Verde. Do not count on seeing them in Europe, however. Only six frigate birds have been sighted there since 1852!

Puffing out the large red bag under its throat, a male courts his female. He stands on the spot where the nest will be built in the colony and spreads his wings to display himself to the potential mate. Their nests are usually built in the undergrowth or, less frequently, on a rock face.

Like its cousin the cormorant, the frigate bird possesses a powerful long curved beak which it uses to hassle and intimidate other sea birds as they fly by. Frightened and bullied by pecks from this beak, the latter drop the fish that they have caught, saving the frigate bird the trouble of having to go and find them itself.

Like living clocks,
crabs
change colour according to the time of day

Living in colonies at the water's edge, fiddler crabs come out of their holes (a long tunnel of a metre or two in length dug in the sand of the beach) to look for food.

A veritable migration begins at low tide, when the sea goes out, leaving behind on the shore the small organic debris that the crabs like so much.

THE CHAMELEONS OF THE CRAB WORLD

Some crabs have also mastered the art of changing colour. The crabs of the mangrove swamp, which includes species of the genera Uca and Grapsus, use colour as a means of communication between the sexes. To attract a female, the fiddler crab (Uca) can change colour in a few minutes. The famous naturalist Darwin himself noted this phenomenon in 1874: the white and green male of a South American species, of which the female is a grey-brown colour, can become even more brightly coloured, just like a chameleon. These colour changes are often accompanied by lively movements of the pincers.

During the mating season, the male fiddler crab (here, *Uca tangeri*) is brightly coloured.
In order to attract the female's attention further, the Uca begins waving its pincers around in an exotic dance routine.

The male fiddler crab, identifiable by its abnormally large pincers.

A DIFFERENT COLOUR FOR EVERY HOUR

Most fiddler crabs also change colour according to the time of day. These crabs have a body clock that is set by the time of the tides: at low tide, the colour of their brown feet fades and their shell becomes darker. In some species it becomes blue, whilst in others it turns orange and white. Only the colour of the pincers, which differs according to the species, remains unchanged during this 'makeover'.

This species of the genus Eucarcinus is one of the few to live several kilometres from the sea. Caught in a downpour, these crabs are able to take shelter in a tree, making this also one of the few climbing species. On a moonlit night, females migrate in large numbers to the sea where they lay their eggs.

Grapsus grapsus seem to cover every square centimetre of basaltic rock in the Galapagos Islands. In their hundreds, these crabs feed on the seaweed found among the rocks, eating the small scraps caught in the cracks.

Trying to get close to one of these stunning Grapsidae demands great patience, and the speed with which it flees makes photographing it extremely difficult. These crabs have feet in the form of 'brushes' which they use to rake the sand as they look for food.

Grapsidae prefer rocky habitats. Among these, the red *Grapsus grapsus* lives on the reefs around the Galapagos Islands.
It is the most common species of crab on the islands and, according to visitors to the islands, unquestionably the most beautiful.

Creative workshop

Having studied all of these creatures,
it's time to get creative.

All you need are a few odds and ends and a little ingenuity,
and you can incorporate some of the animals we've seen
into beautiful craft objects.

These simple projects will give you further insight into the
animal kingdom presented in the pages of this book.

An original and simple way to enjoy
the wonderful images of the animal kingdom.

Parrot rucksack

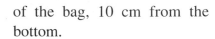

*B*righten up a rucksack with the vibrant colours of the parrot. This motif could also be used on a cushion or other fabric item. Use fabric offcuts.

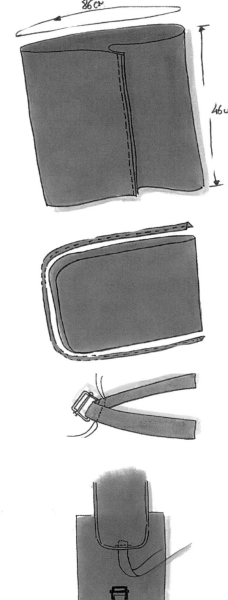

Making the rucksack

• Bag: cut a rectangle, 86 cm by 46 cm. Fold in half along long edge, right sides facing, and sew the edge.

• Flap: cut a rectangle 28 cm by 68 cm. Fold in half along long edge, wrong sides facing. Cut two corners curved. Cut a 96-cm length of bias binding, and fold in half lengthways. Sew around three sides of the flap.

• Shoulder straps and fastening straps: cut two strips of fabric 80 cm by 8 cm, and two strips 20 cm by 8 cm. Fold each strip in half lengthways, right sides facing. Sew along the whole length, reverse and sew up the ends.

• Straps to close flap: cut two strips of fabric, one 20 cm by 8 cm and one 10 cm by 8 cm. Complete in the same way as shoulder straps. Sew the large strap to the underside of the flap. Fold the small strap around the third buckle and sew it to the centre

of the bag, 10 cm from the bottom.

• To sew up the bottom of the bag: turn the bag inside out. Slide the fastening straps inside. Align them with the edges of the bag, about 8 cm from the side and sew along the bottom edge of the bag and over the ends of the straps.

• To attach the shoulder straps and the flap to the bag: place the unbound edge of the flap and the unsewn ends of the shoulder straps on the back of the bag (not the side with the strap to attach the flap), 5 cm from the top edge. Sew into place.

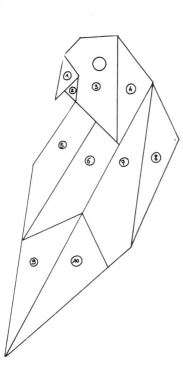

• To close the bag: create a hem 2 cm deep around the top of the bag. Thread the cord through the length of the hem.

Making the parrot

• Photocopy the design for the parrot, increasing its size by 20 times. Cut out the pieces to make templates.

• Place each template, wrong sides facing, on the chosen fabric. Draw round the template, and cut the material 5 mm wider than the template.

• Sew the pieces of fabric together in the following order: join pieces 1 and 2, then pieces 3 and 4, then join these to make the head; join pieces 5 and 6, then pieces 7 and 8, then join these to make the body; join 9 and 10 to make the tail, then join all three large pieces together.

• Handsew the parrot on to the flap of the rucksack and glue a felt circle on to the parrot to form the eye.

Iron the whole bag.

This motif could also be sewn on to other fabric bags, or on to a cushion cover.

Materials

• 1.10 m of green fabric (width 1.20 m) • thread • 1.5 m of green bias binding (5 cm wide) • scraps of fabric in various colours • three buckles • 1 m of cord

Chameleon pencil-holder

M*ake a colourful rainbow with this chameleon pencil-holder*

Cutting out the sections

Photocopy the drawing of the chameleon, increasing it to the size you prefer.

Place two pieces of thin cardboard (a little larger than the

size of the chameleon) on top of each other and tape together.

Place the photocopy on top of the pieces of thin cardboard and tape on top of the cardboard pieces.

Cut out the design with a Stanley knife.

Preparing and painting the chameleon

Coat the top and edges of each chameleon shape with plaster of Paris, using a paintbrush.

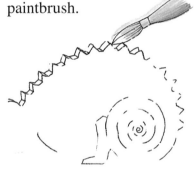

Leave to dry, then rub the front and edges with sandpaper.

Spray the shapes, front and back with green acrylic paint,

then paint the backs with yellow, giving a mottled effect.

Preparing the polystyrene

Cut the polystyrene in the shape of the chameleon, but 1 cm shorter so that it will not show when assembled.

Paint the polystyrene and the

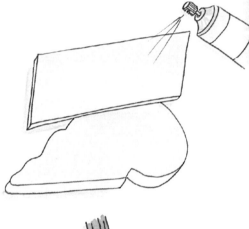

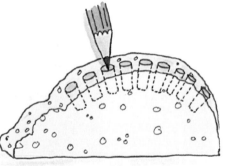

base, using the yellow spray paint.

Once the paint has dried, make about ten holes in the top edge of the polystrene, using a pencil. These holes will be used to hold pencils or pens.

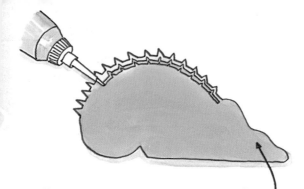

Decorating the chameleon

Decorate one side of the chameleon using glitter glue or acrylic paint.

Glue the two beads together and then on to the cardboard to make the eye.

Assembling the chameleon

Glue one cardboard chameleon on to each side of the polystyrene block, and glue the whole thing on to the cardboard base.

Materials

• a sheet of thin cardboard • a piece of very thick cardboard 20 cm by 6 cm for the base • a piece of polystyrene or foam • adhesive tape • 2 cans of acrylic paint in green and yellow • 10 coloured pencils or paints • very strong glue • a green bead and a blue tubular bead of the same diameter as the green bead • plaster of Paris • a Stanley knife • fine sandpaper • paintbrush

Origami animal boxes

*I*n Japan, folding paper is an ancient art. These coloured animal boxes can be used in the office (for paper clips, elastic bands etc.) and in the home (for jewellery, pins and so forth).

Preparing the paper

Cut out a square of tracing paper, at least 25 cm by 25 cm.

Paint the tracing paper using a paintbrush.

Once the ink or paint has dried, flatten out the paper and fold as shown in the diagram.

Completing the boxes

Stick animal stickers on to the sides, and varnish the whole box.

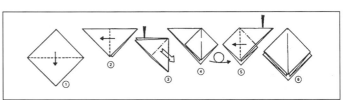

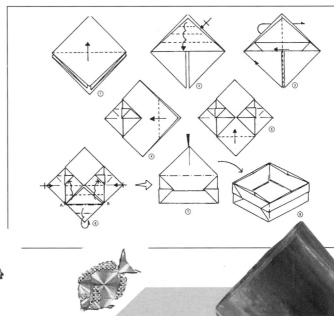

Materials

• tracing paper • ink or paint in two colours
• animal stickers • clear varnish • paintbrush

Peacock coffee-filter holder

*U*se the peacock's stunning plumage in your kitchen to keep your coffee filters close at hand. A project for woodwork enthusiasts.

Preparing the pieces

Photocopy the design, increasing the size so that the template for section C is 12 cm high. Use the same percentage increase for the other templates.

Place the templates on the plywood (glue the reverse of the template on to the plywood or attach with sticky tape) or draw the shapes directly on to the wood.

Clamp the plywood on a table or workbench and carefully cut out pieces A, B, C and two copies of piece D with the jigsaw.

Sand two bevelled sides on piece E (following the angle of piece A) and the bottom of the two D pieces. Pierce a hole with the gimlet (for attaching the coffee-filter holder to the wall). Sand all sides of the other pieces.

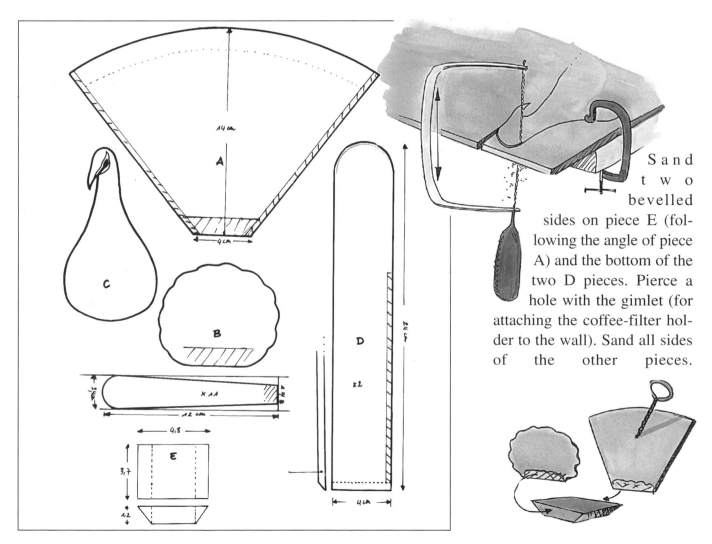

the strip of wood. Sand the 'feather strip' by turning it against the rotating disk of the sander, following the curve drawn. Then sand both sides of the strip. Repeat for the other ten feathers.

Feathers

Saw the strip of wood into 11 pieces, each 12 cm long. Draw a circle 2.5 cm in diameter at one end of each piece, and two diagonal lines.

Set up the sander and insert

Assembly

Spread neoprene glue on to the bottom of pieces A and B and the front and back edges of piece E, 1.2 cm from the edge. Wait for two minutes and then assemble by putting piece E between the other pieces (see diagram) and pressing down for one minute.

Spread glue on the base of the two D pieces 1.5 cm from the edge, and on the two bevelled edges of piece E.

Repeat the process on the side

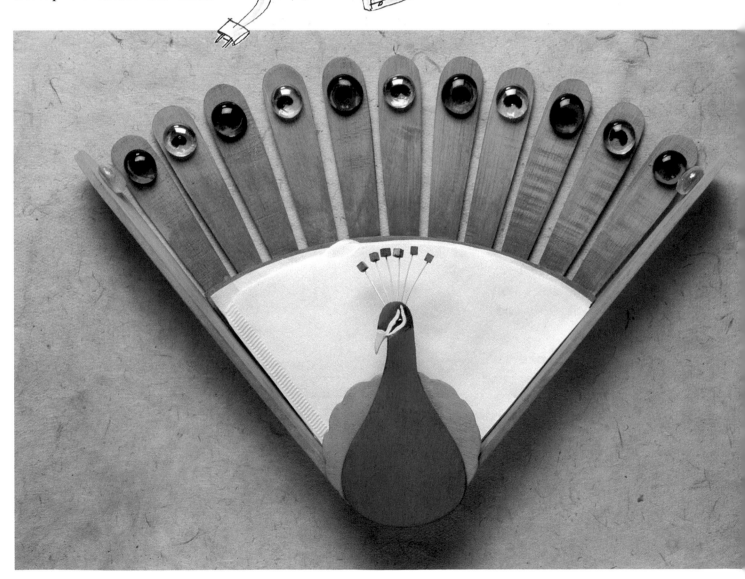

edges of piece A and 2 mm along the two D pieces.

Turn the glued section over, and spread glue on the back of piece A, 2 cm from the curved edge.

Spread glue 2 mm from the bottom of each of the 11 feathers.

Wait for the glue to dry and place the feathers at regular intervals. Press down for one minute.

Sand the whole piece, removing excess glue.

Painting

Dilute some of the pale green paint, and paint the feathers on both sides so that the grain of the wood shows through.

Paint the rest of the bird with undiluted paint of the same colour.

Paint the body of the peacock in blue-green. Following the picture, paint the beak yellow, and the eye black and white.

Headdress

Using the pliers, cut three pieces of wire 10 cm long. Fold each piece in two. Fold each end back by 3 mm. Put a blob of strong glue on to the end of each, and thread a bead on to the end. Repeat for each feather.

Glue the three wire pieces behind the peacock's head, sticking a piece of sticky tape over the back so you can press down on the headdress without sticking your fingers to it!

Put neoprene glue on the back of the peacock (not the head) and on the central part of piece B. Leave to dry, then assemble.

Materials

• a 20 cm by 30 cm offcut of plywood, 3 mm thick • a 5 cm by 6 cm piece of wood, 12 mm thick • a strip of thin wood 2 m long, 2.5 cm wide and 1. 5 mm thick • 2 clamps • a sander, and sandpaper (rough and smooth) • neoprene glue • acrylic paint in yellow, turquoise, pale green, black and white • 30 cm of white wire • a small tube of strong glue • 13 coloured-glass circles • six small blue beads • a jigsaw (hand or electric) • a 4-mm gimlet • medium and fine paintbrushes • a pair of pliers • a black pen • a ruler

Photographic credits:

Colibri: E. Janini: 69a; A.M. Loubsens: 54a, 54c, 56a; J.L. Paumard: 41b; J.M. Prevot: 68b

Nature: 21b; Anagnostidis: 16-17, 18, 33, 45, 46c; H. Chaumeton: 12-13, 19, 28c, 30, 58a, 59, 78b, 79b; Chaumeton/Lanceau: 21a, 24a, 19b, 31b, 32a, 46a, 46b, 47, 60b, 69b, 71, 78a; J.P. Ferrero: 67b; Franco Bonnard: 36b; Gohier: 27b, 48b, 50a, 50b, 52a, 79, 80b; Grospas: 22b, 25b, 44/45; Krasnodebski: 48c, 49b; Lanceau: 14a, 15, 20a, 20b, 28a, 28b, 29, 49a, 53a, 62a, 62c, 63a, 68a, 68c, 70; Louisy: 60a, 60c, 61; Mayet: 13, 14b, 26a, 66a, 66b, 67a; Paul Meitz: 67c; NHPA Dalton: 37; Polking: 17, 36a, 38, 39, 76a, 76c, 77, 80a, 81; Prevot: 23, 48a; A. Reille: 27a, 62b; Revy: 25a; Samba: 6b, 63b; F. Sauer: 22a, 24b, 26b, 31a, 32b, 34, 35, 58b, 58c, 64a, 64b, 65a, 65b, 76b

Okapia: M.U.H.D. Dossenbach: 50c; Natur im Bild/R. Förster: 51; B. Roth: 53b; A.J. Stevens: 52b

Géry Parent: 72a, 72b, 72c, 73a, 73b, 74, 75

Phone: Beste H & J/Auscape: 55b; Jean-Paul Ferrero : 54b, 55a, 56b, 57; J.P. Ferrero/J.M. Labat: 10; Pascal Goetgheluck : 11b; François Gohier: 8-9; Labat-Jardel: 40a, 40b, 42-43; Raymond Valter; 9a, 11a, 41a

Acknowledgements

The publishers would like to thank all those who have contributed to this book, in particular:
Antoine Caron, Michèle Forest, Céline Gerst, Rizlane Lazrak, Nicolas Lemaire,
Hervé Levano, Marie-Cécile Moreau, Kha Luan Pham, Vincent Pompougnac,
Marie-Laure Sers-Besson, Valérie Zuber, Emmanuelle Zumstein

Illustration: Franz Rey
Translation: Michael Mayor, Sarah Snake

Printing: Eurolitho - Milan
Dépôt légal September 1998
Printed in Italy